TIMELESS TRIBUTE

Arrangements for the Early Advanced Pianist
by Marilynn Ham

CONTENTS

Lillenas Publishing Co.

KANSAS CITY, MO. 64141

To Sandy, with thanks and appreciation for all her time, talents and care.

Timeless Tribute

Regal, slow

Arr. by Marilynn H

"The God of Abraham Praise" (Hebrew Melody)

A little faster

mp

cresc. poco a poco

Tempo as before

rit.

f

Slower ♩ = 76

*El Shaddai (Card / Thompson)

molto rit.

8va

una corda

Delicate and
very expressive

p

begin accel.

"A Mighty Fortress Is Our God" (Martin Luther)

ff   faster ♩ = 120

more quickly   lighter

With all my love to my daughter, Meryl Joy

A Child of the King

with *I'D RATHER HAVE JESUS*

JOHN B. SUMNER
Arr. by Marilynn Ham
Expressive

Tenderly ♩ = 76

With ped.

For Lona

Rock Medley

Arr. by Marilynn Ha

"The Solid Rock" (William B. Bradbury)

Lightly, happily ♩ = 112
"He Hideth My Soul" (William J. Kirkpatrick)

For Uncle Bill and Aunt Frances

Were You There?

with *CROWN HIM WITH MANY CROWNS*

Arr. by Marilynn Ham

*Bass octaves to sound like nails driven, death, finality.
**Use of the left hand enhances the voicing of this duet and allows for a singing legato tone.

* "Were you there when they laid Him in the tomb? . . ."

* "Were you there when He rose up from the grave? . . ."

Briskly
"Crown Him with Many Crowns" (George J. Elvey)

In gratitude to Robin and Janet

Holy, Holy, Holy

JOHN B. DYKE
Arr. by Marilynn Har

To Roscoe, for his godly example and friendship

Victory in Jesus

with *PENTECOSTAL POWER*

EUGENE M. BARTLETT
Arr. by Marilynn Ham

30

♩ = 132
*"Pentecostal Power" (Charles H. Gabriel)

32

For Jody, who comes to mind often when I play this

Great Is the Lord
with MORNING HAS BROKEN

MICHAEL W. SMITH and
DEBORAH D. SMITH
Arr. by Marilynn Ham

36

*Arr. © 1987 by Lillenas Publishing Co. All rights reserved.

Quickly, in one (♩ = 152)

40

To my Aunt Muriel and her family, for all their love and support

Worship the King

(A Christmas Medley)

♩ = 112

Arr. by Marilynn Har

"Hark, the Herald Angels Sing" (Felix Mendelssohn)

Excitedly ♩. = 76
*"Worship the King" (Smiley, George)

Thinking of fond family memories—with Dad, Mom, and my fourteen brothers and sisters

Wonderful Grace of Jesus

HALDOR LILLENA
Arr. by Marilynn Ha

For Lyndell Leatherman, my editor and friend

Jesus, Lover of My Soul

with *LIKE A RIVER GLORIOUS*

SIMEON B. MARS
Arr. by Marilynn Ha